Hollywoodn't

Thanks! We'll be in touch

Behind the curtain: a life of struggle, triumph, and laughter!

Written By Kent Kasper

Table of Contents

Opening

When I started writing this book, I called it "170 Ways to Be Rejected as an Actor." As I delved deeper into the project, I realized that my initial concept only scratched the surface. Although humorous in hindsight, the rejections I'd collected over the years had once caused me significant heartache, disappointment, and frustration.

With 20, 30, and even 40 years of reflection, I now see the humor in these experiences. Many of the casting professionals I encountered had attempted to soften the blow of Rejection with creative, often humorous, feedback. Their efforts to camouflage the harsh reality of my performances during those early years are now comical.

As an actor with thousands of auditions under my belt, it's impossible to recall every experience. However, around 170 rejections have stuck with me, and I've realized how hysterical they are as well as insightful.

The saying goes that "comedy is tragedy plus time." These rejections were tragic at the moment, but with time, they've become comedic gold. I've explored the concept of Rejection more deeply, moving beyond just the humorous anecdotes.

My 40-Year Journey as an Actor

I began writing this book twenty years ago, but life's priorities took over. Celebrating my 40th year in acting made me realize the value this book could bring to thousands of aspiring actors. Many face the harsh reality of relentless Rejection, leaving them on the verge of quitting and fearing lifelong regret.

The odds are daunting: With 320 million people in the US and only 189,000 union actors, 80% of whom are often unemployed, my acting teacher's words still resonate with me: "If you have something else to do, get out. If not, sit down and commit." While most of my classmates left, I stayed committed.

Throughout my 40-year journey, I've battled self-doubt, confusion, disappointment, and anger. There have been times when I considered quitting and going back to practicing law or stand-up comedy. As a child, I thought getting on TV was effortless, but I've since learned the harsh realities. Acting is a marathon, not a sprint.

Thousands of aspiring actors arrive in major entertainment markets such as NYC, LA, and Atlanta every day, chasing their dreams. The challenge lies in securing jobs, navigating obstacles, and managing nerves. Often, family and friends lose faith. Despite my acting and comedy credits, recognition has eluded me.

After 40 years in the industry, I've come to value small victories— landing jobs, coaching, and feeling fulfilled. While fame may or may not be mine, I'll continue dancing and stay in the game.

As long as I am breathing and above ground, I have faith that a door will open, and I will stick my foot into it and never let it close.

I'll never forget the advice Chuck Woolery, the beloved game show host who sadly passed away yesterday, shared with me during a commercial break on the TV show "Love Connection." We chatted about his journey to Hollywood, where he initially aspired to become a country-western singer inspired by George Strait. However, he struggled to get noticed and was on the verge of returning home.

Fortunately, his agent began securing auditions for game shows, leveraging Chuck's tall, handsome presence. He took on these opportunities to support himself and his family. Over time, Chuck achieved recognition, fame, and fortune, establishing himself as a renowned game show host for decades.

I asked Chuck for advice, sharing that I had only recently arrived in LA. He offered these wise words: "You can spend your whole life knocking on the front door, but if the side door opens, put your foot in and never take it out. You never know when those doors will open again."

In this book, I'll share my personal experiences and insights on handling Rejection, using humor as a tool for resilience. As an actor and coach with 18 years of experience guiding others through the audition process, I've developed a unique perspective on coping with Rejection.

Today, with the rise of self-tape auditions, the dynamic has shifted. Casting professionals' immediate feedback and polite rejection comments are mainly absent. While I've adapted to this new landscape, I miss the comedic aspects of in-person auditions.

This book is my attempt to share the "sausage-making" process and give readers a glimpse behind the curtain. I hope that new and seasoned actors alike will find humor and solidarity in these stories, that they'll come away with a deeper understanding of the unpredictable nature of our craft, and that non-actors will get a clearer understanding of what it takes to pursue such a path.

Bradley Cooper once shared remarkable insight in an interview. As a young actor, he realized that his job was to act and that his chances of landing a role were extremely low. So, he approached every audition with a mindset shift: he assumed he wouldn't get the job. Instead, he focused on enjoying the process of acting. He was thrilled to have the opportunity to showcase his craft, and any positive outcome was a welcome surprise.

Other actors, including Michael Keaton and Steve Carell, have echoed similar sentiments. They noted that once they accepted the low probability of booking a job, they began to view auditions as a chance to share their passion for acting. They recognized that casting directors had sifted through thousands of submissions to select them for an audition – a victory!

As an acting coach, I emphasize to my students that getting an audition is a triumph. It means they've beaten out 99% of the competition, and their odds have improved dramatically. I encourage them to celebrate this achievement and understand that landing the job is beyond their control. Instead, they should focus on giving their best performance and "leaving it all on the field."

By grasping the mechanics of the acting business and acknowledging the daunting odds, actors can find joy in the process, even in the face of Rejection. As Cooper and other renowned actors have demonstrated, a mindset shift can transform the audition process into a liberating and enjoyable experience.

I am constantly reminded of this age-old story when I think of all the rejections I have gotten as an actor over the last 40 years.

Many years ago, a determined gentleman embarked on a daunting task. With a suitcase full of vacuums, he set out to sell them door-to-door, driven by the responsibility to provide for his family.

For 12 grueling hours, he knocked on door after door, facing Rejection and dismissal at every turn. Many slammed their doors, telling him to leave. Despite the discouragement, he persisted, knowing his family's well-being depended on his success.

Just when he was about to give up, exhausted and disheartened, he knocked on one final door. To his surprise, it opened, and he was invited in. This customer not only purchased one vacuum but also bought his entire stock.

Overjoyed and relieved, the gentleman returned home to his family with enough money to pay their rent and put food on the table. His perseverance had paid off, and he was grateful for the lesson learned: that with determination and persistence, even the most demanding challenges can be overcome.

Chapter 1

From Rejection to Resilience: My 40-Year Journey in Acting, Comedy, and Law

For 40 years, I've navigated the cutthroat worlds of acting, comedy, and law. Despite accumulating hundreds of rejections, I've persevered, driven by an unwavering determination to succeed.

As a stand-up comedian, I faced tough crowds and eventually became a sought-after national headliner. As a lawyer, I secured a coveted position as a New York City Assistant District Attorney. However, I also faced academic Rejection, failing the bar exam 12 times in three different states.

In the acting industry, I've faced overwhelming odds. To cope, I've tried various tactics to get noticed, from changing my appearance to creative audition strategies. Some worked temporarily, but ultimately, they were short-lived.

This book isn't a guide to acting success or a rant about industry flaws. It's a candid, humorous reflection on the relentless rejection actors face.

Initially, Rejection felt like a bullet to my soul. But five years in, something shifted. I realized Rejection wasn't the enemy; it meant I was still in the game. I adjusted my mindset: "I'll probably be rejected, but I'll have a great time anyway."

This liberation from disappointment allowed me to accept Rejection as a natural part of the process. I learned to view Rejection as fuel, not failure.

Key Takeaways:

1. Rejection is an inevitable part of the acting journey.
2. Taking it personally can be devastating.
3. Shifting your mindset transforms Rejection into a driving force.
4. Acceptance and resilience are essential for success.

My story is a testament to the human spirit's capacity for growth and perseverance. This book, I hope, will inspire and empower aspiring actors to navigate their craft's challenges, never taking Rejection personal. Taking Rejection personally is like a mental cancer that will start out as confusion and disappointment and slowly metastasize to frustration and grief, eventually poisoning your spirit and soul with anger and rage. Once you stop taking Rejection personally, the journey of becoming a working actor and wading through the endless and nonstop rejections becomes joyful and, in many ways, comedic.

Chapter 2

Early Struggles with Rejection

As a young actor, I struggled intensely with Rejection. I became obsessed with my perceived flaws whenever I didn't land a role. Was I too tall, too Jewish, too skinny, or too fat? Did I need to gain talent, intelligence, or style? I felt inadequate, believing Rejection was a reflection of my self-worth.

This toxic mindset ravaged my emotional, physical, and spiritual well-being. It strained my personal and romantic relationships, impacted my finances, and affected where I lived. Rejection became cancer, poisoning my system and worsening my spiritual turmoil with each audition and subsequent Rejection.

Knowing that 99% of auditions end in Rejection, I realized I needed a drastic mindset shift. Faced with the prospect of abandoning acting for law or comedy, I understood that unless I transformed my perspective, Rejection would ultimately destroy my passion and career...

Chapter 3

From Desperation to Inspiration: My Journey to Empowering Actors

Eighteen years ago, my acting career had stalled. Despite having multiple talents as an actor, writer, stand-up comedian, and attorney, I felt lost. The scarcity of roles and constant disillusionment left me desperate for a new path. That desperation made me discover my passion for coaching actors in branding, marketing, and packaging.

Fellow actors ridiculed me, saying, "You're not a household name; who'll come to you?" However, 18 years later, I have proven them wrong, and I have coached and mentored hundreds of actors on resilience and transforming Rejection into a positive force.

Through thousands of rejections and auditions, I've become an expert in navigating the emotional turmoil that comes with Rejection. I teach my students that Rejection isn't personal and that every "no" brings them closer to booking a role.

Pursuing acting is not for the faint of heart. With only 179,000 union actors in the US and 80% earning below the poverty level, it's a challenging and competitive field. My advice to aspiring actors is simple: if you can walk away without a second thought, then do. But if the passion for acting haunts you, stay in the game.

Denzel Washington's words echo in my mind: "The ghost of missed opportunities will haunt you." Rejection is inevitable, but it's not insurmountable. I empower my students to face rejection head-on, persevere, and transform it into fuel for their success.

Hang around the barbershop long enough, and you're bound to get a haircut.

"Denzel Washington"

Chapter 4

Favorite one-liners about my decades of facing Rejection as an actor:

1. "Rejection is my middle name. Luckily, it's also my agent's."
2. "I've been rejected so many times, I've started thinking my headshots are actually 'no' shots."
3. "My acting career is going great – I've mastered the art of rejection!"
4. "Thousands of rejections? No problem! I'm just pacing myself for that Oscar acceptance speech."
5. "My agent says I'm a talented actor. The trouble is nobody else agrees... yet!"

6. "Rejection is just redirection... to another audition, and another, and another."

7. "Auditioning is like dating – mostly disappointment, occasional false hope."

8. "Every 'no' brings me closer to that glorious 'yes'... or so I keep telling myself."

9. "My rejection collection is impressive – I'm considering starting a rejection museum."

10. "When life gives you lemons, make lemonade. When life gives you rejections, make a highlight reel."

Here are some more one-liners about facing Rejection as an actor:

More One-Liners

1. "Rejection is my superpower – I can handle it faster than Spider-Man can swing from skyscrapers."

2. "My acting resume is 90% rejection, 10% determination.

3. "If at first you don't succeed, destroy all evidence that you tried."

4. "Rejection? No worries! I'm just stockpiling material for my future Oscar acceptance speech."

5. "I've got 99 problems, and rejection is all of them."

6. "My agent says I'm 'almost there.' Almost where? I'm not sure."

7. "When they say 'no,' I hear 'not yet' – or sometimes just 'no.'"

8. "Rejection? Just another chance to practice my 'I'm still confident' face."

9. "Auditions are like pizza – even when they're bad, they're still pretty good."

10. "Rejection isn't failure; it's just pre-acceptance."

11.   "If rejection were money, I'd be a millionaire by now."

12.   "My favorite word? 'Next!' – as in, the next audition."

13.   "I've mastered rejection; now I'm working on perfection."

14.   "Rejection is like a bad haircut – it'll grow out eventually."

15.   "No doesn't mean never; it means 'not now, try harder.'

Chapter 5

A Powerful Mindset Shift for Actors

I still recall Michael Keaton's insightful words from one of his videos. He shared how a simple, yet profound mindset shift transformed his approach to auditions and, subsequently, his entire acting career.

Initially, Keaton would get nervous, upset, and depressed about auditions. However, he had an epiphany that changed everything: he realized that auditions weren't about Rejection but about someone wanting to see him act. If they liked him, they'd bring him back and pay him.

This mindset shift is a game-changer. By viewing auditions as opportunities rather than threats, Keaton was able to approach them with a sense of excitement and curiosity.

Embracing the Odds

Statistically, actors face Rejection a staggering 98-99% of the time. However, as the old proverb goes, "One yes trumps many nos." It doesn't matter how many times you get rejected; one "yes" can change everything.

Even after 40 years in the industry, when I audition, I'm no longer attached to the outcome. I give it my all, leaving everything on the table. I know nobody can outdo me in terms of passion and dedication. They may outshine me, but they can't out-kent me.

Rejection in the acting world can be brutal. The emotional toll is overwhelming, causing heartbreak, disappointment, and spiritual poisoning. Physically, it can manifest in headaches, stomachaches, and strained relationships.

"When you are starting out you need to act everywhere you can. You can't be picky! If you get a chance to act in a room that some else has paid rent for then you are given a free chance to practice your craft and in that moment you should act as well as you can .So if you leave the audition and you acted as well as you can then there is no way the people who have watched it will forget it. Always back to the moment where you need to act as well as you can."

Phillip Seymour Hoffman

Phillip Seymour Hoffman's advice is about making the most of every opportunity when starting out as an actor. I would break it down like this:

1. **Be opportunistic:** Take every chance to act, regardless of the setting or production quality.
2. **Don't be picky:** Early in your career, it's not about being selective; it's about gaining experience and honing your craft.

3. **Treat every opportunity as a chance to practice:** Whether it's a small, low-budget production or an audition, give it your all and use it as a chance to improve.
4. **Focus on the present moment:** Instead of worrying about the outcome or future opportunities, concentrate on delivering your best performance in that moment.
5. **Leave a lasting impression:** If you've acted to the best of your ability, you'll be memorable to those who watched you, increasing your chances of future opportunities. Hoffman's advice emphasizes the importance of being proactive, taking risks, and focusing on the process rather than the outcome.

Once an actor understands this every single audition, they ever go to is no longer poisoned by fear of Rejection but rather the rainbow of opportunity and a chance to practice their craft.

Chapter 6

The Power of "Booking the Room"

Rejection can be a blessing in disguise. Instead of viewing it as a failure, consider it an opportunity to lay the groundwork for future success. This concept is what I call "booking the room."

"Booking the room" means making a lasting impression on decision-makers, even if you're not the right fit for the current opportunity. Think of it like being an apple when they're looking for an orange. You may not be the perfect match, but your unique qualities make you memorable and worthy of another look.

I've experienced the power of "booking the room" firsthand in my acting career. After auditioning for the TV show "Monk"16 times, I finally landed the role on my 17th attempt. What seemed like 16 rejections were actually 16 opportunities to leave a lasting impression.

This mindset has helped me cope with disappointment and Rejection. Instead of focusing solely on booking the job, I emphasize booking the room – giving my best performance and making a lasting impression.

Key Takeaways:

1. Rejection can be a steppingstone to future success.
2. Focus on impressing decision-makers with your unique qualities.
3. Don't get discouraged by immediate Rejection; it may lead to future opportunities.
4. Leave a lasting impression, and you'll increase your chances of success down the road.

By adopting this mindset, you'll learn to reframe Rejection as a natural part of the journey to success.

The Key Takeaways from 40 Years of Rejection offers valuable insights into the impact of Rejection and how people cope with it. Here are the key takeaways:

Rejection's Impact:

1. **Mental Health:** Rejection can lead to anxiety, depression, and low self-esteem.
2. **Physical Health:** Chronic Rejection can weaken the immune system, lead to cardiovascular disease, and affect sleep patterns.
3. **Relationships:** Rejection can damage relationships, erode trust, and lead to social isolation.
4. **Overall Well-being:** Rejection can affect self-worth, confidence, and overall quality of life.

Chapter 7

Comedic Relief:

My Funniest 170 Rejections

1. **Humor as a Coping Mechanism:** People use humor to diffuse tension, hide their true feelings, and make Rejection more bearable.
2. **Witty Rejections:** Some individuals use humor to soften the blow of Rejection, making it easier for the recipient to accept.

Patterns in Rejection

1. **Niceties and Euphemisms:** People often use polite language and indirect phrases to avoid hurting someone's feelings.
2. *Identifying Patterns:* Recognizing these patterns can help individuals prepare for Rejection and develop strategies to cope with it.

By understanding the impact of Rejection, recognizing the role of humor in coping, and identifying patterns in Rejection, individuals can better navigate Rejection and develop resilience.

However, amidst the devastation lies a comedic goldmine. The ridiculous ways people sugarcoat their Rejection can be laugh-out-loud hilarious. Casting directors and industry professionals try to soften the blow, often resulting in silly responses.

My Favorite Actor rejections of all time in my 40 years as an actor:

1. "Pull the tall, bald guy in black rim glasses off the set. He's too prominent."
   Over 100 guys dressed in business suits who resembled me are all bunched together... suddenly I heard a megaphone... next thing you know, I was gone...

2. "They thought you did a great job, but they decided to go with a real amputee."
   Only then did the realization hit me like a ton of bricks that having all my body parts and limbs was going to hurt my chances of being cast? I considered cutting off my right leg only to realize that hoping the rest of my life to auditions wasn't a very good option.

3. "So, how is your agent, Helen? I thought she passed away a few years ago."
   Sometimes, having a D-list agent is like not having an agent at all.

4. "Do you know the last time you auditioned for me; you left a giant black footprint on my wall?"
   Years later, the same CASTING Director sent this to me. I knew my audition was pretty violent and forceful, but I didn't realize when I kicked my boot into the wall that it would leave such a gaping hole and a lasting impression for over 30 years... She never brought me back in for another audition. The moral of the story is "If the construction crew has to come in after your audition, it probably didn't go very well."

5. "Tough break... Sorry, the producer used the waiter from his favorite Italian restaurant."
   The next day, I went to the same restaurant and submitted my application to be a part of the waitstaff.

6. "That accent of yours, is it Boston or British?"
   Well, at least they both began with a B.

7. "Being 6 foot five is going to cause you lots of problems. Ted Danson and Tom Selick are exceptions."
   Suddenly, I was pissed and wished my mother had an affair with a short mailman.

8. "You made some great choices."
   None of which was to become an actor.

9. "I missed the boat before and passed on a lot of great actors, but I'm going to have to pass on you. I may end up regretting it."
   Forty years later, I'm sure this agent hasn't lost a second of sleep over not signing me.

10. We already have too many of you."
    Decades before the term "doppelgängers."

11. "Your role as floor waxer almost got upgraded to principal, but the client decided it wasn't critical to the plot."
    Man, oh, man! It certainly felt critical to the plot based on the two words I had in the script.

12. "They want to book you as a corpse. You will have to be facedown."
    Memories of my last two honeymoons.

13. "They don't want to show your face."
    Suddenly I am in the "witness protection program ".

14. "I see you teach Traffic School. I just got a speeding ticket last week."
    Here we go again...

You wash my back. I wash yours.

15. "The scene works better if you don't throw yourself against the wall; besides, you were out of frame when you dropped to the floor."
Suddenly, the casting director becomes Steven Spielberg.

16. "I feel terrible that you flew all the way from New York City to Los Angeles. The role of the farmer really wasn't right for you."
I guess the pitchfork was a little over the top...

17. "You don't need to smile. You are a print body double, and your head will be cut off anyway."
Talk about being invisible...

18. "The priest is midwestern. Could you do it and sound less New York and less Jewish."
Is this an audition or a KKK meeting?

19. "The producers decided to go a different way for the role of the mailman. They thought you looked too educated."
Tough to dumb down 5 years of post-graduate work to look like a civil servant.
"Do you still practice Law?"
Game over!

20. "Please don't turn your face to the camera. The director only wants to film you from the back or silhouette."
The $45 I spent buying theatrical makeup wasn't the best investment.

21. "Your read is a bit over-the-top. The show is called Judging Amy, not Judging the Prison Guard ".
Oh, sorry, sometimes I forget to pass the ball rather than shoot it!

22. "Great job. What kind of car do you drive?"
Extra! Extra! Read all about it!

23. "You didn't need to bring the telephone receiver to the audition. Miming it would've just worked out fine."

Those were the days when I brought more props to an audition than Carrot Top.

24. "You remind me of Woody Allen, but you sound like Howard Stern."
One man is 5 ft 5. The other is 6 ft 5.

25. "Was that a southern accent I just heard?"
Earning a living as a voice-over artist is out of the question.

26. "Is that an accent you are putting on, or is it some sort of cartoon voice? If you wouldn't mind, could you please use your real voice?"
Maybe I should've been born during the silent film era.

27. "My staff finds you to be very irritating, and the messages you leave are really annoying. I'm gonna be dropping you."
Can you kindly be more direct?

28. "You are very physical. Do you have a dance background?"
6 foot 5 inches and 295 lbs. Do I look like a ballerina?

29. "It's okay; memorization is not important. Would you like to take a moment?"
As the ship is sinking, a life raft is thrown my way.

30. "Would you do extra work? The back of your head may be usable."
This gives new meaning to adding insult to injury.

31. "Great job, but how many 6 foot five 275-pound bald men with a goatee do you see as bellhops?"
One, but he was mentally challenged and an ex-convict.

32. "Great costume. Looks so real."
Happy Halloween, everybody!

33. "Would you wait outside? My associate and I need to talk something over with my staff. Okay! You can leave now."
Yes, it's anonymous.

We all think you stink.

34. "Hey, thanks for coming in. You are great, but I won't be needing your picture."
I want to forget you even existed from the very second that you walked out the door.

35. "You did a great job in front of the producers, but we brought you in 3 to 4 times already. Let's take a break for a while."
You're like a bad herpes sore -you just keep coming back.

36. "You are fabulous. I just love you. I really love you. I shouldn't be saying this so soon, but I love the way you look and the way you sound.
Is this casting director trying to book me or trying to F me?
I didn't book the role of this casting director, and he didn't bring me back for over 25 years.

37. "Nice job... do you have a tuxedo? By the way, do you know how to waltz?"
What the hell is going on? What am I? Suddenly, Gene Kelly and Fred Astaire!

38. "Hey, wait a minute. Aren't you one of the BALD guys? You are better actors and less dandruff. That was so funny."
The whole office was laughing a few months back when we got your card, thinking how desperate actors can be. Now, seeing you in person only reaffirms what an idiot you are.

39. "Will you do nudity?"
Serves me right responding to a casting in Screw Magazine.

40. "You are perfect!"
Game over!

41. "Terrific, you are very tall."
That's a wrap, folks!

42. "You are great. Are you available next week? I really don't need to see an adjustment. I've seen enough. Have a good day."
Zero-paying job or deferred pay.

43. "Did you get the script the other day?"
And the fat lady has just sung.

44. No need to say "scene "when you're finished. We know when it's over."
Acting class mistake 101.

45. "We loved you, but we went with the name."
We had a name attached before you ever woke up this morning.

46. "When you say, 'it's time,' it means he's being released from jail. Your read sounds like he's going to the electric chair."

Don't count on even being brought in again until the apocalypse ends the world.

47. "Really appreciate you coming in on such short notice."
And wasting our time and your gas money.

48. "We don't shake hands. It's a germ thing."
This was 25 years before Covid.

49. "Would you consider being a stand-in for the actor we just hired?"
You suck, but you look like the actor we hired who has talent.

50. "Thanks. We will keep your picture on file for future projects."
Maybe in the year 4020.

51. "You are hysterical! You should try stand-up."
What am I a clown?

52. "You're too over the top ...The director likes it real."
And Jim Carey isn't?

53. "Wow, that was great. It was like watching a play."

What you really mean is that it is more like watching paint dry.

54. "Great voice! Have you ever considered doing voice-over work"
    Talk about wasted wardrobe choices.

55. "That's all I need to see. Thank you."
    Your audition made me projectile vomit.

56. "Could you wait outside? The producers have narrowed it down
    to the three of you. The one we book will go over to the set now.
    Okay, you're released".
    Get the hell out of here!

57. "Do you still keep your legal license?"
    You're going to need it after that horror show.

58. "So, are you still a member of the California bar?"
    Because, as an actor, you can't get arrested.

59. "Is your California bar card current.?"
    Better renew it if you know what's good for you.

60. "What does your family think about you leaving the law?"
    Do they think you're as big an asshole for doing it as I do?

61. "It makes no difference that you were really a lawyer. Legal shows
    choose the guy who can act like a lawyer. Maybe you should try to
    get work as a legal consultant."
    Dam, I can't even act like a Real Lawyer...

62. "Leave your telephone number with us. We will be calling people
    over the weekend."
    The check is in the mail, and I promise I will pull it out.

63. "So when are you going back to New York City? Oh, I'm sorry, I
    didn't know you live out here."
    And once you leave my office, I will forget you ever existed.

64. "It's between you and another guy. Keep your fingers crossed."

50-50 chance. There is a 100% chance it will be the other guy

65. "You are on avail."
Only if you leave town and book a nonrefundable ticket will you book this job.

66. "You are on serious avail."
We're pretty damn serious. You're not gonna get it.

67. "You have the right to first refusal."
But don't get your hopes up; I don't think you're gonna be refusing anything.

68. "You are the director's first choice."
Right behind his gardener, nanny, and babysitter.

69. "You are off of avail."
Get the noose ready.

70. "You have been pinned."
And it ain't the prom season pal.

71. "You've just been released."
Suddenly I feel like I'm on the set of Shawshank Redemption.

72. "The producers decided to go a different way."
Path that leads in a lot of directions, but none of which is to you.

73. "So, how do you support yourself?"
It certainly is not through acting.

74. "The writer was in the room. They didn't appreciate you changing their words?"
He cursed your existence before you even got to your car.

75. "You don't recognize me? You were a Maître D' at a restaurant when I was a waitress."

Here is a perfect example: karma can take 40 years. I was a host at a restaurant, and I treated this waitress like shit and gave her the worst tables, paid her no mind, and basically treated her like crap. Well, it turned out she was the main Casting Director for LA Law. She called me in for an audition. I didn't remember her at first, but I just knew the memory I had wasn't good. Well, needless to say, I never got the job, and she got her revenge.

76. "Have you considered taking a workshop?"
And not walking in here, embarrassing yourself, and wasting my time.

77. "Do you study with a coach?"
If so, that coach sucks.

78. "The client decided to go with the younger dad, sorry."
It's the guy he had sex with at the ski resort.

79. "It's amazing how much you look like our executive producer. Good luck to you."
The most despised guy on our production team.

80. "A little advice: unstaple your script. It's easier to turn the page and doesn't make so much noise. Very distracting."
Game over!

81. "Your picture is going right on top of my callback pile."
Then, directly in the garbage pail.

82. "You should feel proud of yourself for memorizing all that."
After all, a trained monkey could've done what you had just done.

83. "I know you're reading for the role of the dentist, but it's not necessary to put your fingers so close to my mouth."
We thank the heavens you weren't auditioning to be a proctologist.

84. "The TV show was shot in Toronto. They can get local actors for co-star roles. They can't afford to fly LA talent in."

And trust me, even if they had the budget, you wouldn't see the inside of an airport.

85. "Kent Kasper. Fabulous name!
Now, get the hell out.

86. "The producers loved you. Next time, they'll bring you in for the meatier role. You're way too good for this one."
If they had to take a lie detector test, the machine would have blown up in their faces...

87. "Oh, my goodness! You're the guy that sent me that BALD phone card. Such a great idea. Everybody in the office was laughing. It's still in my wallet. Let me show you. Thanks for coming in."
We were all laughing, thinking how absolutely desperate you were doing something as dumb as this. You give a brand-new name to "pathetic."

88. "You were the producer's first choice for the role of Colonel Klink. They loved you, but they made an offer to a well-known character actor."
It looks like the monocle I bought, the German army outfit, and the riding crop would be my next Halloween costume.

89. "Sorry, they didn't think you looked enough like a lawyer."
I guess being an ex-assistant, district attorney and graduating law school wasn't enough to convince you. Oh well.

90. "Respond okay, ready when you are. Okay, go ahead... Anything the matter? Action! Probably a good idea to use a script.
Here, I froze like I was being held up at gunpoint at an ATM machine.

91. "The casting person doesn't remember you. I know you show-casted for him six times but he sees so many people and he is really bad with faces. Can you please fax him your picture?
We threw out our fax machine eight years ago.

92. "Do you normally wear makeup to auditions?"

I guess the red rouge on my cheeks was a little bit much.

93. "The casting director won't see you for her show. She remembered you from that date you had with her 10 years ago. I guess it didn't go very well."
Once again, karma came to bite me in the ass 10 years later. I had taken this girl out for a date. It didn't go very well, and I don't think I was very nice. Well, as it turns out, she was casting a hit-network television show. Again another casting director got their revenge on me, Karma baby, Karma.

94. "You didn't book your role of the lawyer, but they offered you the part of the Hasidic rabbi. No words, just mumbling prayers."
Believe it or not I took the gig it and it was for LA Law. We shot it on a stormy night at 20th century Fox. Myself and nine extra rabbis mumbling Jewish prayers around the table dressed like extras in a Woody Allen movie.

95. "It's no surprise with all the personal problems Woody Allen has been having that your part would've ended up on the cutting room floor."
My luck. I play a perv directed by one.

96. "The script was running long, so they decided to cut the role of the tourist."
How in god's name can this production continue now.

97. "Odds are the hotdog vendor won't be upgraded."
What a shocker!

98. "I have some bad news for you...The producers who booked you for the role of the racist Maitre' D lost their funding. Sorry, the project is dead."
They were recently arrested at a KKK rally.

99. "I'm sorry, you were really great these last two days of rehearsals, but the producers feel it's just not the right fit. No need to return tomorrow for taping"

Two days were plenty to see that you a lousy actor. Now return your wardrobe and parking pass and get the hell out or we call security.

100.   "Why in God's name did you spray real perfume during your audition? Casting just called my office screaming that their staff is coughing and that everybody following your audition is also feeling ill. You are fired!"
My agent called me right after this and told me I was fired.
It could have been worse. I could've been auditioning for an assassin...

101.   "Why the hell did you bring your friend to the shoot? He was attempting to massage and adjust the three Oscar-winning actresses and heckling them during the shoot. Don't you know it was a closed set! You are fired!"
I brought my idiot friend with me, who was a massage therapist and eventually became a chiropractor. Boy was I an idiot. The agent fired me the next day. Talk about bringing an idiot to work!

102.   "They cut the role of the ringside doctor. We were looking forward to working with you. The director said he'll call you in on his next project."
Or when the world explodes into a zillion little pieces.

103.   "I'm sorry we won't be filming your scene. No, not tomorrow, either. The director has cut it. If you wouldn't mind, could you remove all your valuables from the trailer now?"
The police are on their way to escort you off the lot.

104.   "Your segment may only be seen in the UK."
Or if you're lucky on the moon.

105.   "You won't have any lines; there's going to be voice-over to your actions."
And Charlie Chaplin just called. They want you on the set Asap.

106.   "If Boston wins, your spot will run ...If Chicago wins, the spot will run ...If both Boston and Chicago win, the spot runs."

Sorry Yanks and the Marlins in the World Series. Your spot is shelved.

Heads, I lose. Tails I lose.

107.   "The client had bought 1600 spots for your commercial, but the legal department screwed up and gave final approval to Miss Moore. She stopped it dead in its tracks. This one would've won a Cleo."

This one truly broke my heart. I booked the role of Murray, the famous character on the Mary Tyler Moore show. We shot it at Universal Studios. It was an absolutely magnificent commercial. They said it would win all sorts of awards and would run for a year. The legal department screwed up on this, and they didn't procure the rights, and it never ran. This one truly broke my heart. Even 35 years later, it still kills me.

108.   "So sorry they wrote your character out at the last minute, but they promised to bring you back for something else."
It's more likely that I have a drink with Moses and Jesus and then see these people again.

109.   "So sorry you've been downgraded. They can't afford you."
Suddenly, I am Brad Pitt

110.   "Your spot won't be running. It didn't test well."
Just like my SAT scores.

111.   "Kent, sorry, the print job for the medical brochure has been canceled for tomorrow because the client has not made up his mind about whether they want to do it or not. You are off hold, bye."
Now get the hell out, loser.

112.   "You're wonderful. Probably the most fun three days of shooting that we've ever had. Unfortunately, the client decided to go more serious."
Suddenly I am Bozo, the clown.

113. "Tough break. You were a sure bet to be upgraded in the airline spot. Unfortunately, the client decided to scratch the "talking seat premise."
Darn, I thought I would win an Oscar for the "talking seat."

114. "They wanted to book you, but they thought you'd be difficult to work with."
Get in line!

115. "The client saw you sleeping on the front lawn during lunch. That's very unprofessional. I will not be sending you out again."
Hey, it was a 6 am call. What do you expect?

116. "What in god's name were you thinking when you brought your friend with you to the photoshoot? I got reports that he annoyed the photographer, bothered the caterer, and made dumb jokes about your bar mitzvah during the actual shoot with three Oscar-winning actresses. You are fired!"
I guess I confused the day with "bring an idiot to work."

117. "The star of the series is tall, so they went with a short co-star."
I called the surgeon after the audition and got a price check on how much it would be to amputate my legs.

118. "You look too Jewish."
Suddenly, I am a Rabbi.

119. "Your name is not Jewish enough."
I went directly home after this and got the paperwork to legally change my name to Moskowitz.

120. "They decided to go ethnic."
I went directly home and changed my passport name to Jesus Gonzalez.

121. "We decided on a woman."
I went directly home and contacted a surgeon to find out about what it would take to become a post op tranny.

122. "They decided to go younger."
This was long before Botox, unfortunately.

123. "They decided to go older."
Feel free to call me Daddy.

124. "They decided to go more "Middle America."
Suddenly, I am on the set of Leave It to Beaver.

125. "They decided to go shorter."
I am 6 feet 4

126. "They decided to go heavier."
Fk me.

127. "They decided to go thinner."
Fk me.

128. "We decided to go bigger."
6 foot 4 290lbs. What are you looking for, Hulk Hogan?

129. "They decided to go more Blue-collar."
Then call Jeff Foxworthy.

130. "We decided to go more White collar."
Okay, I will call the manager of CVS to come in and read it for you.

131. "I'm sorry, but the producer decided to go with a guy with more hair and a name."
Strike 2

132. "Anyone ever tell you look like Mel from the Dick Van Dyke show?"
He is bald and dead.

133. "You remind me of that German guy on Hogan's Heroes."
He is bald and dead.

134.   "Would you shave?"
My nuts, maybe.

135.   "Shaved head and a goatee. You are limiting yourself to bad guy roles."
Tell that to someone who gives a flying s...t.

136.   "Have you ever considered shaving your head and growing a goatee? It would give you a better chance at booking bad-boy roles."
How about I cut off my penis instead?

137.   "Have you ever considered wearing a hairpiece? It would make you look 10 years younger."
Die!

138.   "What about a mustache?
Suddenly I am Grouchy Marks.

139.   "You look like a seedy insurance salesman with a mustache.
That's the role, you dumb putz.

140.   "Do you wear glasses? Ever think about contacts?"
What the hell are you my optometrist?

141.   "Without glasses, you look washed out."
The last time I looked, I wasn't an albino.

142.   "That is an absolutely hysterical wig. Where'd you get it?"
That's the last time I bought a toupee from a TV guy advertisement.

143.   "You look much younger in person."
Suddenly I morphed into Benjamin Button.

144.   "Your pictures don't do you any justice."
Thank you, I'll be sure to tell my friend, the court reporter who drew them.

145. "Couldn't tell how tall you were from your headshot."
You're not supposed to! Idiot! it's a damn picture, not a hologram.

146. "My goodness! You're a big fellow. Ever play basketball?"
Wait a minute, I'm 6 foot four, not 7 foot four. What the hell is the matter with you?

147. "Man, you're a big guy. Have you ever played football?"
Yeah, when I was six.

148. "They thought you were just too big. They were afraid you would divert attention away from the stars of the show."
It's not my fault every actor in a soap opera is as tall as a lawn jockey.

149. "Is that a Russian accent? To be honest, it sounds kind of like Yiddish."
Take your pick.

150. "Is this a lithograph? A photo reproduction may be a better way to go."
That was the last time I ever printed my picture off my home computer.

151. "I see that you're a nail-biter."
It's better than being a compulsive nosepicker.

152. "The producer thought your head was too well-shaped. The star's head is more banana-like."
I thought about running home and putting my head in a vice.

153. "You never paid me a commission on the hundred dollars you won on the game show. Pay me and then we're finished."
My very first agent was in Los Angeles. She wanted a commission from a dopey game show.

154. "Do your glasses have any lenses in those frames?"
Maybe I shouldn't have paid extra for those special lenses that they call non-reflective.

155. "You don't have any credits."
And I get the feeling that I won't have any additional credits either after this audition.

156. "You don't have enough credits."
I bet you don't say that to Meryl Streep.

157. "Your only credits are co-star credits."
Well, they considered me for a role on Friends, but unfortunately, it was to play a tree.

158. "You don't have any guest star credits."
Allow me to apologize for not being John Hamm.

159. "I don't see any series of regular or recurring guest star credits on your résumé."
Oh no. I was wondering why I had to pay $25 to park on the lot.

160. "No offense, your résumé reads "day player". There's no money in that. A day or two of work here and there, that's it."
Oh, sorry about that. Before I forget, please allow me to apologize for being born.

161. "Your résumé reeks of being an extra."
Excuse me, I'd rather you call me by my right name, Atmosphere or Background.

162. "Casting directors are gonna look at your résumé and see you as a comedian, and not as an actor. We won't be able to help you."
That didn't work for Ray Romano or Jim Carrey, did it?

163. "Your name needs to be more Jewish."
Excuse me, sir, my mother's great great great uncle was a rabbi.
Kent Bradley Kasper sounds like a wasp.
Suddenly, I am Ryan O'Neal In Love Story.

164. "We are going to have to take a pass, Kevin."
Thanks, but my name is Kent.

165. "Thanks for coming in, Keith."
Excuse me, my name is Kent.

166. "It's nice to have met you, Kenny."
My name is Kent.

167. "That was a great read, Kurt."
Thanks, that was my father's first name.

168. "Have you ever considered changing your name to Jackie Balloons?"
Yeah, at the same time, I was considering running away and joining the circus.

169. "Are you in class now?"
Game over!

170. "My producer was furious when she received a subpoena, especially since she was going through a divorce. She cut her vacation short, flew back, and met with her attorney. Her reaction was intense: Are you out of your mind? What you did will get you blacklisted in Hollywood!".

I thought I had come up with a clever casting promotion. As a former assistant district attorney in the Bronx, I had some old subpoenas that I doctored to look like casting notices. However, they still resembled real subpoenas. I put them in envelopes, and when people received them, they thought they were real subpoenas. Unfortunately, my plan backfired. The casting director and several others were livid and threatened to blacklist me. I was forced to take out an ad in Variety, where it said, "Kent Kasper apologizes for the unnecessary use of a subpoena." It was embarrassing, but I learned a valuable lesson. At the time, I thought my idea was genius, but in hindsight, it was a mistake.

Chapter 8

Vanishing Victories

As an actor, I've experienced my share of disappointments. Even when I've booked a role and beaten the odds, there's always a risk that the project won't come to fruition or that I'll be edited out.

I recall booking a role for a Carefree gum commercial, which was slated to run for years and potentially win a Cleo award. However, the legal department failed to clear the rights, and the commercial never aired.

Another disappointment was when I booked a CBS pilot and spent three days filming on set. I had my own trailer, parking spot, and wardrobe. However, when I received a copy of the pilot, I was shocked to find that my scene had been cut.

I also booked a role in a Woody Allen movie, "Husbands and Wives." I was thrilled to work with my idol and filmed my scene in front of Bloomingdale's. However, due to controversy surrounding Woody Allen, my scene was cut from the final version.

Additionally, I booked a role in the original "Space Jam" movie as the team doctor. I spent the day on set, dressed in my doctor's outfit, but was unexpectedly told to go home without filming my scene. The movie went on to run for 30 years, and I was never seen in it.

My subsequent major disappointment occurred while filming an IBM commercial. I had the opportunity to work with a highly acclaimed director, but unfortunately, our experience together was less than ideal. Despite his reputation, I found him to be challenging to work with.

I had high hopes for the commercial, thinking it would be widely aired and provide me with a significant payday, possibly even enough for a down payment on a house. However, the commercial never ran. Sometimes commercials are tested with focus groups and don't perform well, but I never found out why this one wasn't aired.

I was left feeling disappointed and frustrated, having celebrated the initial victory of booking the job only to have my hopes dashed once again.

I booked a commercial for Microsoft, which I thought would be a national success. However, just before it aired, I was informed that my role had been cut. The commercial ran for months, but I was nowhere to be found.

Another massive acting disappointment came after booking and shooting a Mercedes-Benz commercial. The shoot lasted three days, and I had my own parking spot, a trailer with a shower, and two days of wardrobe fittings for the 1950s retro-themed piece. I even became friendly with the producers and directors. The location was absolutely stunning.

However, over two months passed, and the commercial hadn't aired. Then, I was at a friend's house when I recognized the music and exclaimed, "Here comes my spot!" But when the commercial played, I wasn't in it. I asked my friend to replay it, thinking I might have missed myself, but I was nowhere to be found. It felt like I had never been part of the production at all.

To add insult to injury, I was only paid for a few days of work, despite the commercial running for almost three years. I later found out that the other actors made hundreds of thousands of dollars, while I earned a few thousand dollars. That experience hurt, both financially and emotionally. It was a tough one to get over.

These experiences have taught me that even when you've achieved success, there's always a risk of disappointment.

Conclusion

As a seasoned actor with 40 years of experience, I've navigated the entertainment industry's highs and lows. While rejection has been a constant companion, it's only part of my story. With hundreds of commercial bookings, dozens of TV shows, film roles, music videos, industrials, voiceovers, and print campaigns under my belt, I've enjoyed my fair share of successes. One of my most lucrative gigs was a Lending Tree commercial, where I appeared on screen for less than a second. Despite the brief appearance, the commercial ran for over four years, earning me over $250,000 in residuals. I've also showcased my comedic and stand-up skills on top talk shows, including Jimmy Kimmel, Jay Leno, Conan O'Brien, Pat Sajak, Joan Rivers, and David Brenner. In addition to my acting work, I've appeared on reality shows, dating shows, and game shows. I've been an imposter on a gay psychic show, a world-renowned window washer, and a whistler show. I've also done my fair share of dating shows, including "The Connection" in 1994. One of my favorite experiences was working on a prank show called "Prank My Mom." I played various roles, including an egotistical producer and one of the world's worst dates for women. Also, I spent twenty years as a celebrity lookalike for a top television personality and was a stand-in and double for a Hall of Fame NFL quarterback. I've also had my share of unconventional experiences, including being kicked off the set of

Family Feud. After seven hours of being passed over, I'd had enough and let the producers know how I felt. They didn't take kindly to my outburst, and I was escorted off the lot. In addition to my acting work, I've had a successful 20-year run as a national headline stand-up comedian, performing at top venues and appearing on notable TV shows. I've also held the converted position of Assistant District Attorney in The Bronx District Attorney's Office, beating out over 20,000 applicants for 44 spots by jumping up on the conference table and doing three minutes of stand-up comedy during my fifth and final interview for the district attorney's office. The past 18 years, I've added being a successful branding, marketing, and acting coach, as well as an audition specialist. to my life as an actor. Coaching and mentoring have brought me a great sense of satisfaction and fulfillment as I've been able to make a positive impact on people's lives. It also pumped new life into my acting career giving me a greater sense of purpose. Up until the time I started to coach the biggest thrill I got was booking a job, but once I started coaching and mentoring, I got an even bigger thrill and satisfaction when I helped one of my actors land a job...They say being of service to others is what defines your life and gives It meaning. My 40 years in the entertainment industry have been an emotional rollercoaster, but my passion for the craft has never wavered. For me, auditioning is exhilarating – a chance to showcase my skills, take risks, and experience the thrill of the unknown. I hope my story can inspire others to pursue their passions, even in the face of rejection. A great actor once said" The only thing more difficult than booking a job as an actor is selling poetry door-to-door" Looking back. I'm pretty darn fortunate to have sold my share of poems. Looking ahead. - I'm pretty confident I will sell a few more.

Made in the USA
Las Vegas, NV
15 December 2024

14417979R00028